THE WHOLE THING

The Story of the Bible
Through Six Images

Jason English

Illustrated by Belle Hissam.

ISBN: 978-0-578-49244-5
Hardback IBSN: 978-0-578-50667-8
Ebook ISBN: 978-0-578-49286-5

Unless otherwise noted, all biblical passages referenced are from the New International Version.

DEDICATION

To Kimberly,
      You are my best friend, my wife,
      and my teacher.
      You are the matriarch of a new way of living
      in the kingdom;
      My queen of the meadow that leads me into
      the forest.

To my daughters, Grey and Violet,
      You are both so strong and wonderful.
      Thank you for your love.
      I'm so lucky that I get to be your dad.

I love diving as deep as I can,
into a topic or story or theme,
swimming around,
holding my breath,
feeling the silent power of stillness,
and emerging to the surface,
with one little shell or starfish,
that will somehow,
demonstrate the whole ocean,
to the one who receives it next.

CONTENTS

FOREWORD

"I wish the Bible came with an instruction manual," she said. I was her pastor. She was in recovery – from a toxic, fundamentalist upbringing that emphasized how bad she was, how bad the world was, and how very mad God was. She needed some good news.

The Whole Thing is good news. It's not a step-by-step instructional manual, but it is a wise guide to faithful engagement with God's Story. In it, Jason reveals that the Story is not fundamentally about brokenness, but wholeness. As it turns out, God isn't waiting to catch you or trick you or berate you, but longs to guide you into the mystery of Love. You'll see that the "Good Book" is, indeed, a very good book!

Jason is a master teacher. In his writing, the complex is made simple. As he reveals the deep structure and direction of the Story, the reader gains access to an interpretive grid that opens her to the way, the truth, the life. As you read, you can almost see the path of wholeness opening before you. Wholeness is what it's all about. It's the divine DNA imprinted on reality. No wonder neurobiologists and physicists are now discovering what poets and mystics have long been saying – everything is whole, everything coheres at the most fundamental level! Jason doesn't use these words, but what he is sharing is a kind of "experiential knowing," a path that is opened as you walk it, a dark night of the soul revealed as redemptive, a journey of unknowing that invites surrender. In six movements with six images.

Jason shows us the whole thing, the unfolding, unifying narrative that both holds and redeems our wild and winding stories.

The Whole Thing will motivate you to explore the Story afresh. I believe it holds the possibility of healing wounded relationships with the sacred text, for healing wounded relationships with the One who writes our stories.

Jason is a teacher who offers fresh insight, but more importantly a teacher who offers transformation – for our whole lives – because he is a pastor who has walked people through painful valleys and because he is a human being who has navigated his own journey with integrity and wisdom. I think you'll read and re-read this one.

- Chuck Degroat, Professor of Counseling and Christian Spirituality at *Western Theological Seminary and Co-Founder* and Senior *Fellow at Newbigin House of Studies.* Author of *Wholeheartedness: Busyness, Exhaustion, and Healing the Divided Self,* as well as several other books.

3

ABOUT
THE ENDNOTES

Instead of placing the references, quotes and song lyrics at the end of the book, I've organized the endnotes so that each chapter is immediately followed by quotes and reading suggestions.

Consider each image's endnotes to be part of the chapter itself.
Let the additional voices inspire you.

Note: There is a short section of the book where you will be asked to read words that are backward. Embrace it.

5

IMAGE 0

God is invisible. Right?

The Bible starts with a very clear purpose. In an ancient near eastern culture, when many nations believed in many gods, there was one group, the Hebrews, who had a different message: that there is only one God. Just One. And this One is not just the One of the Hebrew people, but of everyone and everything.

And this One is seemingly invisible.

What is the narrative of the Bible? What's the *point*? [1]

The Bible is often explained with an overwhelming emphasis on the brokenness of the world.

This book is my wholehearted, simplified explanation of the Bible. I want to explain what I think the whole thing is about. Where it's coming from. Where it's headed. And how the story isn't about brokenness, but wholeness.

This is my attempt to teach the story of the entire Bible in a way that is simple, fresh and memorable. [2]

I'm not trying to explain *everything*. I'm trying to explain the *whole* thing.

––––––––––––––––––––

I want to start with a sense of awe.

The first words of the Bible are found in the first book of the Bible, the book of Genesis. The book of beginnings.

"In the beginning, God created the heavens and the earth."
[Genesis 1.1]

Poetically, many ancient near eastern writings *begin* with specific words or letters for specific reasons. [3]

In Hebrew, the name of the book of Genesis is **Beresheet**, which is also the first word in the book. In our Bibles, it's translated as "in the beginning."

However, there is an interesting Jewish insight regarding the first letter of this first word: the Hebrew letter **Bet.**

The letter **Bet** corresponds to the English letter **B** and is the second letter in the alphabet.

The Jewish rabbis asked the question: *Why do the Scriptures begin with the second letter of the alphabet rather than the first?*
Their insightful answer: *To show that the Scriptures do not answer every question, and not all knowledge is accessible to man, but some is reserved only for God himself.* [4]

Here's what *Bet* looks like:

Bet is closed on the right side but open on the left. Since Hebrew is read from right to left, it appeared to the rabbis that the Scriptures start with a letter that is open in the direction of the reading but closed toward the *beginning* of the text. Something is blocked *before the beginning*. God decided to reveal part of the story, but only beginning with the beginning. Not *before* the beginning. [5]

And so we see that this story has an openness that can teach us. [6]
The Hebrew language is quite interesting in that word images are associated with each letter. In fact, original Hebrew writing used pictographic script (picture representations).

The letter **Bet** is the word image of a **house**.

And in fact, this story is like a house.
The whole thing is a narrative that we live inside of together.
It is a story with boundaries. There are things outside of this house. The outside things are not necessarily contrary to the inside things, but this story is about the inside things that we might begin to comprehend. There are things outside this story, *before things,* that are not told. They remain a mystery to us. And that's ok.

Even in the very first sentence of the Bible, there is no attempt to answer the question of where God himself came from. Many other ancient creation accounts begin with stories about how gods came into existence. [7]

In the Hebrew story, the history of God is a mystery.

Beresheet.

Bet.

Closed on one end and open on the other.
A house that we live in together.

We are invited to start here, in the beginning,
and move forward.

IMAGE 0 NOTES

1 Thomas Cahill is one of my favorite authors. I've learned so much about cultural and historical context from him. In his book, *The Gifts of the Jews*, Cahill explains: "The word *bible* comes from the Greek plural form *biblia,* meaning 'books.' And though the Bible is rightly considered the book of the Western world - its foundation document - it is actually a collection of books, a various library written almost entirely in Hebrew over the course of a thousand years." p.6

2 Ecclesia Bible Society is a collaboration of scholars who gave fresh words to Bible translation. I resonate with their introduction in *The Voice New Testament:* "Our purpose in using these literary devices is to enhance the beauty of the Scriptures and to assist the reader in clearly and quickly understanding the meaning of the text. We are constrained to be faithful to these ancient texts while giving the present reader a respectful and moving experience with the Word of God." p.viii

A similar sentiment comes from Rob Bell, who has a certain way of synthesizing information and getting to the heart of it all. In his book *What is the Bible?* he writes, "If you finished this book and your first thought was *But he left out the passage from the book of _____ that deals with _____,* you're right, I did. I left it out. And there's a very specific reason I left it out: if I didn't, then this book would be called the *Bible.*" p.311

3 I'm so proud of Kent Dobson for many reasons, one being that he wrote a commentary on the entire Bible. I can barely imagine the work that went into that. His *NIV First-Century Study Bible* goes as deep into the Hebrew roots of faith in Jesus as any full-length, single-bound commentary on the entire Bible can. Thank you, Kent.

"Books in ancient times customarily were named after their first word or two.
The English title, Genesis, is Greek in origin and comes from the word *geneseos....Depending on its context, the word can mean 'birth,' 'genealogy' or 'history of origin.'*" p.1

4 I have learned so much from Lois Tverberg over the years. There is an entire section of her book, *Listening to the Language of the Bible,* that first introduced me to the rabbinic analysis of the name of the book of Genesis, as well as teaching me to appreciate the vastness of the unknown.
"There is wisdom in being able to say, 'I don't know and letting God alone know.'" p.64

5 *The Gifts of the Jews* - Thomas Cahill
"He is the God beyond the mountain, even beyond the sky, the unknowable God, whose purposes are hidden from human intelligence, who cannot be manipulated." p.85

6 In his book, *God Was in This Place and I, I did not know*, Lawrence Kushner allowed space for seven different voices to give interpretations of a single passage of scripture. It's a must-read for those who appreciate learning from multiple perspectives.
"Like the One who has no mouth, who spoke the first letter that has no sound, the biblical word conceals an infinity of meanings." p.11

7 *Between God and Man* - Abraham Heschel
The Greeks learned in order to comprehend. The
Hebrews learned in order to revere. The modern
man learns in order to use. To the modern man
everything seems calculable; everything reducible to
a figure. He is sure of his ability to explain all mystery
away. From p.37

IMAGE 1
FINGER

The first five books of the Bible are referred to as **The Torah.**

Genesis. Exodus. Leviticus. Numbers. Deuteronomy.

They are often referred to collectively as **The Law.**

Here's a quick overview of The Torah: [1]

Genesis is the beginning of the story.
The part of the beginning that we have access to.
The beginning of a progressive understanding of
God and of humanity. Humanity had an opportunity
to connect with God in a very intimate way, to walk
with God. But the first humans received
misinformation that made them choose to disobey.
And even though God was everywhere, the intimate
connection became tainted.

There were heroes in the Torah, and yet these heroes
were never able to completely fix that which was
broken. Person after person, main character after
main character, seemed to bring a sense of hope for
restoration. And yet, full restoration never occurred.

Exodus is about freedom. Being set free from
slavery. This is also where *laws* were given.

Leviticus. Remember that year when you said you
were going to read the Bible straight through?
Leviticus might have been where you stopped.

Leviticus is an instruction manual for how to be a priest in God's Tabernacle (a special tent dwelling place of God's presence).

Numbers. If you press through Leviticus, you get to Numbers, the counting of people in different tribes. It's quite thrilling if you give it a chance - or two or three. Maybe more. I can't quite remember how many chances I've given it.

Deuteronomy means *more things*. (Also translated as *Second Law*).

For many of us, the word "law" might not sound like something that would inspire hearts. We might think of the word as meaning "rules" or "stuff we aren't allowed to do." However, in Hebrew culture, **Torah is about God revealing himself to humanity.** The thought of God opening his heart and mind, choosing the risk of revealing previously hidden things; this makes the giving of the Law an act of intimacy. [2]

When God first spoke laws to his people, he spoke them to a man named Moses, who went to the top of a mountain to meet with God while the rest of the group listened from below. It was a holy moment, filled with awe. What I want to focus on is how the moment God spoke, it changed history. It changed everything. Every thing. And if we understand how this changed everything in the course of human history, we may begin to view the Bible differently.

So let's take a moment to appreciate the opening

words of what is sometimes called The Ten Commandments.

"The LORD spoke all these words, saying:"
[Exodus 20.1 NKJV]

Notice the breakdown of this phrase.
The LORD
Spoke
Words
Saying

Who? The LORD.
What? Speaking. Speaking. Speaking. [3]

Before we read what The LORD said, let's appreciate the milestone here. This was the first time in human history (as far as we know) that an entire group of people heard the voice of God. To an ancient near eastern Jew, there are two sections of history: there is before God spoke to us and *after God spoke to us*. (The holiday called *Shavuot* honors this moment. It's also known as Pentecost.)

When God spoke, he didn't start with, "Do better." He started with, "I AM THE LORD YOUR GOD." [Exodus 20.2]

God's first big reveal was that God is the God of the people who were listening to His reveal. [4]

So this Big Reveal started with **identity.**

Identity of God
and
Identity of people.

Here's the next phrase: "who brought you out of

Egypt, out of the land of slavery."
[Exodus 20.2]

God sets people free.
Identity, then action.

The *Ten Commandments* are also called the **Ten Words** or **Ten Sayings.**
The Big Reveal is **ten things.** In Hebrew culture, the idea of there being *ten things* is more symbolic than we might first assume. Ten means...*ten,* of course. But symbolically, ten refers to all ten fingers on one's hands. If you have *ten,* you have them *all.*
Lacking nothing.
The number *ten* evokes fullness. Wholeness.

The One true, invisible God, was making things known.
This is Everything.

The Hebrew culture revolved around this concept. So much so, that the entire school system was centered not only on the initial ten sayings but on the entire Torah, which included hundreds of more sayings. [5]

Our English understanding of the word *Torah* is a bit misleading (this seems to happen quite often, actually). The word *Torah* is usually translated as "Law," but that translation is actually a tiny bit off. The Hebrew word itself means to *instruct,* and the root of this word means *to point in a certain direction.* [6]

Like a finger pointing.

Later, God even carved the *ten things* in stone with his finger.

"When the Lord finished speaking to Moses on

Mount Sinai, he gave him the two tablets of the covenant law, the tablets of stone inscribed by the finger of God."
[Exodus 31.18] [7]

To simply narrow *Torah* down to the basic word "Law," misses the *point*.

Torah means **GO THIS WAY.**

Can you see the image? The Invisible One, Who holds vast amounts of eternal, hidden knowledge, speaks to make something known. [8]

The giving of the Ten Things was the moment God initiated the next part of the story - the story of God setting people free from **the slavery of unknowing.** Let's think about the logic of this moment. God set his people free from slavery, but then they had to figure out what to do next. Where would they go? If they weren't slaves, who were they?

The One true God didn't leave them in a state of unknowing, but spoke instructions to them and pointed the way.

Often, the pointing of the finger can seem like an accusation. This can be a hang-up for some. Maybe you think that somehow this story is about you doing something wrong. To make matters worse, many religious people *do* actively point at others in accusation. This kind of pointing has a darkness to it. (Interestingly, the name *Satan* comes from the Hebrew *HaSatan,* meaning *the accuser.*) But God's story is not the story of a judgmental, religious person. It's a story for former slaves who don't know where to go, so God points the way.

But to where?

Let's go back to the story of a man named Abram (later, called Abraham). This part of the story happened *before* the Big Reveal. Abram lived among a people group that believed in many gods. Then one day, the One true God *spoke* to Abram. [9]

"Go from your country, your people and your father's household to the land I will show you."
[Genesis 12.1]

A land I will show you...So Abram obeyed God and began to walk toward an unknown place.

There is a word that the Hebrew people use for this kind of walking. [10]
The word is **emunah**, meaning **to move toward.** It's a word for the concept of movement without actually knowing where you'll end up. In English, we call it **faith.** When you start to advance in the direction of the thing that you do not yet see, you are exhibiting faith. This sort of movement demonstrates trust. [11]

What was it that inspired Abram's trust? What was he moving toward? He was moving toward a land promised, not just to him, but to generations of his family. God spoke to Abram later saying this:

"Look up at the sky and count the stars
—if indeed you can count them."
Then he said to him, "So shall your offspring be."
[Genesis 15.5]

God gave Abram an immense visual as a way of showing how big Abram's family would be...as vast as a sky full of stars.

In this early narrative of the Bible, we see God presenting guidance, not for the purposes of accusation, but as a way for people to walk forward into unknown territory. God is not against us. God is pointing toward something.
Are we willing to turn and walk toward whatever that is? [12]

Even if we have valid, logical concerns.
Even if we have heavy emotional baggage.
Even if we don't yet know what we're moving toward.

Let's begin to believe.

Let's take a step of faith in the direction God is pointing, even if we don't know how the story will end.

Let's find out where freedom leads and move toward the place that will be shown to us.

IMAGE 1 NOTES

1 Eugene Peterson provided a concise, unrivaled explanation of the first five books of the Bible in *The Message Remix:*

"Genesis is Conception. After establishing the basic elements by which God will do his work of creation and salvation and judgment in the midst of human sin and rebellion (chapters 1-11), God conceives a People to whom He will reveal Himself as a God of salvation through them, over time, to everyone on earth." p.15

"Exodus is Birth and Infancy. The gestation of the People of God lasts a long time, but finally the birth pangs start. Egyptian slavery gives the first intimations of the contractions to come. When Moses arrives on the scene to preside over the birth itself, ten fierce plagues on Egypt accompany the contractions that bring the travail to completion: at the Red Sea the waters break, the People of God tumble out of the womb onto dry ground, and their life as a free People of God begins. Moses leads them crawling and toddling to Sinai. They are fed. God reveals Himself to them at the mountain. They begin to get a sense of their Parent. They learn the language of freedom and salvation." p.16

"Leviticus is Schooling...Everyday life consists of endless and concrete detail, much of it having to do with our behavior before God and with one another, and so, of course, Leviticus necessarily consists also of endless detail." p.16

"*Numbers* is Adolescence. The years of adolescence are critical to understanding who we are…The People of God have an extraordinarily long adolescence in the wilderness - nearly forty years of it." p.16

"*Deuteronomy* is Adulthood…Deuteronomy gathers up that entire process of becoming a People of God and turns it into a sermon and a song and a blessing. The strongest and key word in Deuteronomy is *love.*" p.16-17

2 *God was in this Place & I, I did not know* - Lawrence Kushner. Someday, according to Jewish mysticism, "the entire Torah will be read as one long, uninterruptible Name of God. And that, of course, would dissolve not only the boundaries between the words of the text, but also the boundaries separating reader from text." p.16

3 When I mention "Speaking Speaking Speaking" I must acknowledge Dr. Laura Schlessinger and her book *The Ten Commandments: The Significance of God's Laws in Everyday Life.*

4 *The Gifts of the Jews* - Thomas Cahill.
"YHWH is an archaic form of the verb *to be;* and when all the commentaries are taken into account, there remain but three outstanding possibilities of interpretation, none of them mutually exclusive. First, *I am who am:* the is the interpretation of the Septuagint, the ancient Greek translation of the Hebrew Bible, which because of its age and its links to the ancients bears great authority. It was this translation that Thomas Aquinas used in the thirteenth century to build his theology of God as the only being whose essence is Existence, all other beings being contingent on God, who is Being (or Is-ness) itself. A more precise translation of this idea

could be: 'I am he who causes (things) to be' - that is, 'I am the Creator.' Second, *I am who I am* - in other words, 'None of your business' or 'You cannot control me by invoking my name (and therefore my essence) as if I were one of your household gods.' Third, *I will be-there with you*....which emphasizes God's continuing presence in his creation, his being-there with us." p.109

5 *Meet the Rabbis* - Brad H. Young
First and foremost, the Torah is "a revelation of the nature and character of God...It is not a useless legal code by which no one could ever be expected to live. On the contrary, its teachings give greater meaning to every dimension of a person's life...In Jewish thinking these five books hold a place of distinction in the canon because in them God communicates His tremendous revelation to Moses on Mount Sinai face to face." p.39

6 *Listening to the Language of the Bible* - Lois Tverberg with Bruce Okkema
"The Hebrew word *torah* is derived from the root word *yarah*, which means 'to point out, teach, instruct, or give direction.' *Torah* could best be defined in English as 'instruction,' that is, God's instruction to man." p.9

In English Bible translations, the word torah is typically translated as "law." And although that makes sense within the context of obeying instruction, it does not capture the essence of the word.

For example, the NIV (New International Version) of the Bible translates Psalm 1.2 as: "But his delight is in the law of the LORD, and on his law he meditates day and night."

The (JPS) The Jewish Publication Society of America translates Psalm 1.2 as: "Rather, the teaching of the LORD is his delight, and he studies that teaching day and night." p.10

Do you see how a different view of the same word can change our approach to the whole thing? If *Torah* means "law," we view God primarily as a lawgiver, we may view God as a judge ready to punish us. We then feel as if our primary role is to simply obey in order to avoid the punishment , or else. But if *Torah* means "instruction," we may view God as a loving father teaching his children how to live.

7 Here we get to an incredible part of the story, when God makes himself visible: "Moses said, 'Now show me your glory.' And the Lord said, 'I will cause all my goodness to pass in front of you, and I will proclaim my name, the Lord, in your presence. I will have mercy on whom I will have mercy, and I will have compassion on whom I will have compassion. But, he said, 'you cannot see my face, for no one may see me and live.' Then the Lord said, 'There is a place near me where you may stand on a rock. When my glory passes by, I will put you in a cleft in the rock and cover you with my hand until I have passed by. Then I will remove my hand and you will see my back; but my face must not be seen.'"
[Exodus 33.18-22]

In this passage, we see God describing Himself as having a hand, a face, and a back. Interestingly, "back" is often translated as *shadow* or *where I just was.*

8 *God at Sinai* - Jeffrey J. Niehaus
"The God of the Old Testament is a God who reveals himself. He is also a God who conceals himself." p.17 Niehaus points out that the self-disclosure of God is called *theophany* (from the Greek, meaning *to appear*). "The generous, self-disclosing nature of God is indicated by his appearing visibly to Moses, and also by the fact that He was with Adam and Eve in the garden even after they had sinned." From p.18

9 *The Gifts of the Jews* - Thomas Cahill
Abraham "was to be the father of a great nation, a nation with a singular destiny and a unique role among the nations. For many generations his family, now called the Israelites, passed on the story of their unique destiny, father telling son, mother telling daughter...We find this family - perhaps more than half a millennium after Avraham - in Egypt, where they have become forced labor engaged in building Pharaoh's storage cities but still aware of the old stories of their father Avraham, who talked and walked with their God." p.238

10 *The Heart of a People* - Moshe Avraham Kempinski. God tells Abraham to count the stars, something God himself acknowledges is impossible for Abraham to do. And so it is that "Abraham's descendants are also destined to go into the unknown and attempt the impossible, because that is the essence of their faith." p.18

11 The word *emunah* has the root *aman,* which means to be *faithful*. There is a similar Hebrew word to emunah that shares this same *aman* root. And you already know it. The word is *amen*. It means *Yes. So be it. I agree.*When you move toward the place God is pointing, even when you don't understand, you are saying *yes* to God.

12 *In The Name of Jesus* - Henri J. M. Nouwen
"God is a God of the present and reveals to those who are willing to listen carefully to the moment in which they live the steps they are to take toward the future." p.13

IMAGE 2
HAND

In the next part of the story, a man named Joshua would end up leading the Israelite people farther than Moses could, all the way to the land promised by God to Abraham.

The name, Joshua (**Yeshua** in Hebrew), means *salvation*.
or **God saves.**
or **God is salvation.**

But it turned out that Joshua was just one of many leaders in a series of leaders. These leaders came in the form of judges, kings, priests, and warriors. They spoke powerful truths and helped the people of Israel make important decisions. They were leaders willing to walk in the way of the Lord even when others were not.

But always there was the same pattern:
Collapse, followed by restoration, followed by collapse.
Over and over. Time and time again.

And always there were undercurrents...whispers... stories...anticipations...
a hope of One who would come. A Messiah.

Messiah (from the Hebrew word *Meshiach*) means *anointed one*.

Special. Set Apart. Different. Holy.

An *Anointed One* who would fix that which had been broken.

A Messiah to come and somehow save the people in a way that transcended the failed attempts of the past heroes. The One who would find a way to deliver people who refused to be delivered.

A man named Samson came along. He made a special vow to God. He was strong and helped the nation. Could he be the one? It turned out he wasn't.

A humble shepherd named David became a powerful king. He was an unbelievable leader, a king who loved God. And even though he brought about more unity than ever before, he also failed in some extreme ways. He wasn't the one. *But* there was something about King David that touched the hearts of the people in a significant way.

And so a nickname was formed for the coming Messiah: The Son of David. One who would come from the family line of David, who would do what no one else could do and restore everything.

But when? How? Who would this Messiah be? And how would they know it was him?

In the meantime...during the waiting, the cycle continued.
Hope built. Hope destroyed. Repeat.
Why wasn't anyone able to break the cycle?

In the midst of these whisperings and hopes were the Prophets (*Nevi'im* in Hebrew). [1]

Prophets spoke from God, about God.
What they said was true. And what they said *came* true.

If those claiming to be prophets spoke something that *wasn't* true, or if their predictions didn't come true, they were called *false* prophets...
almost as if they were pointing the wrong direction.
True prophets were sent by God specifically to speak about God in terms of his relationship to people. [2]

And they were...*quirky*.

They created tension through a dualistic experience, often in the form of performance art.

There was the *form* of what they were doing
(their actions)
and the *content* of the message (their words).

Form
and content.
Actions
and words,

with a purposeful disconnect. [3]

The prophets spoke regularly of **the hand of God.**
They would even speak of feeling God's hand at work in and through themselves.

They spoke of power and strength because of God's hand.

Prophets like Ezekiel, Ezra and Isaiah would say things like:
"the hand of the Lord was on me" [Ezekiel 37] [Ezra 7] and
"This is what the Lord says to me with his strong hand upon me" [Isaiah 8]

It's as if the prophets themselves *demonstrated* the hand of God to the world. And they did so in ways that didn't always make sense.

This
                    created

tension,

but it was certainly memorable.

———

Prophets challenged the culture.
They were known for *doing* and *saying* extreme things. [4]

The prophet Ezekiel made a clay model of the city of Jerusalem and destroyed it to show that the city would be destroyed. At one point, he cooked bread over a fire, using excrement as the fuel. [Ezekiel 4]

Isaiah prophesied naked for three years. [Isaiah 20]

There was **form** and there was **content**.

Extreme **warnings** and extreme **hopes**. [5]

Prophets spoke dramatic messages of a day when God will pour out his Spirit on all people [Joel 2].

They said that people had to turn from their evil ways. [Jeremiah 35]

They declared that God would have compassion by defeating sin and hurling it into the depths of the sea. [Micah 7]

They spoke of the specific birthplace of the promised Messiah. [Micah 5]

They said, "the earth will be filled with the knowledge of the glory of the Lord as the waters cover the sea." [Habakkuk 2]

The common word associated with the prophets was the Hebrew word **teshuvah**. In the English language, we translate the word *teshuvah* as **repent**.

It means to **remember** and **return**. [6]

Remember. Almost as if we have a collective memory of the way things were before things got shattered. And a collective memory of walking somewhere new, together.

Return. A call to turn around and walk in the direction we were going.

It's easy to forget, isn't it?

It's easy to forget where you're going, especially when you don't know exactly where that is.

The people were supposed to be following
the way that
the finger was pointing.

But instead, people stepped off of the path, going a different way.

People forgot where they were going.

**And the prophets were there,
as the hand of God,
pushing people back onto the path.**

Guiding. Pulling. Pushing. Reaching.

Sometimes gently. Sometimes not.

The message was, over and over, to walk straight. Not left. Not right. There is no other way to go than The Way.

Don't forget. Keep going.

The prophets demonstrated the hand of God, returning people to the path of instruction from God (where the finger was pointing).

The finger simply pointed the way, and if someone were to simply turn around and walk in the way the finger pointed, they would no longer feel accused.

They would simply...see where to walk.

Turning around, in order to know where to go.
This is **repentance**.

Prophets were men and women who held up
mirrors to the people, showing them how **backward**
things were.
In essence, saying:
You are going in the wrong direction. Would you just
turn around and begin again to walk in the way the
finger is pointing?

In the prophetic writings, the hand of God was a
symbol of creation and strength.

"Has not my hand made all these things, and so they
came into being?"
[Isaiah 66]

Eventually, there was *another* image that became
common:
The *right hand* of God.

"My own hand laid the foundations of the earth,
and my right hand spread out the heavens."
[Isaiah 48]

OK. Now we're getting more specific. It's one thing
to refer to God's finger, and even his hand, but to get
specific enough to refer to his *right hand*.
Now this invisible God is becoming more...*personal*.

The seemingly invisible God somehow actively, personally and visibly engages with creation. He used his hand to lay the foundations of the earth. He used his right hand to spread out the heavens. At this point in the ancient near eastern culture, the right hand of a leader was considered to be an extension of that leader. The highest ranking official sat at the right hand of a king, as the king's representative. A son sat at the right hand of a father to receive a blessing.

And so the *right hand of God* became associated with the promised *Messiah* - God's highest-ranking official. God's representative. God's son.

The seemingly invisible God apparently has a Right Hand that demonstrates His visibleness. The one who was promised to restore everything is **the same one** who spread out the heavens. The coming Messiah was there at *the beginning*.

Could it be that the one who was promised to *restore* everything is a
visible version
of the one who *made* everything?

The prophet Isaiah said "the Lord himself will give you a sign: "The virgin will conceive and give birth to a son, and will call him *Immanuel*." [Isaiah 7.14]

Immanuel means **God with us.** [7]

God
With
Us

And so hope sprang up.
A Maybe.

Maybe the Messiah would be the one who would let them know what the finger was pointing to.

They waited for the Messiah.
They waited for a very, very long time - through times of war and times of peace, through seasons of starvation and seasons of plenty.

But the hand of God was always there.
And still is.

HOLD THIS PAGE UP TO A MIRROR

The hand of God is here.
Even when we forget.
Even when we've been hurt.
Even when people misuse the words of God.
Even when we step off of the path.

"Whether you turn to the right or to the left, your ears will hear a voice behind you saying, "This is the way; walk in it."" [Isaiah 30.21]

Let's embrace the strong hand of God that pulls us back onto the path. Let's keep walking together, even when our hearts ache. Let's turn around and begin again to walk toward what we cannot yet see.

"Come, let us return to the Lord. He has torn us to pieces but he will heal us; he has injured us but he will bind up our wounds. After two days he will revive us; on the third day he will restore us, that we may live in his presence. Let us acknowledge the Lord; let us press on to acknowledge him. As surely as the sun rises he will appear."." [Hosea 6]

Let's remember and return.

IMAGE 2 NOTES

1 *Between God and Man* - Abraham J. Heschel
"It is predominantly the experience of the *transcendent* God whose voice speaks to the living and finds an echo in their hearts that forms the core of prophetic consciousness." p.17

2 *The Prophets* - Abraham J. Heschel
"The theme of prophetic understanding is not the mystery of God's essence, but rather the mystery of His relation to man....He never discloses the life of the beyond, but always speaks of an appearance, God as turned towards man." p.620

3 *Teaching as a Subversive Activity* - Neil Postman & Charles Weingartner
Neil Postman wrote a lot about the need for a shift in the way we educate. And although this idea didn't originate with Postman, this is the book that introduced me to the concept that "the medium is the message." p.17

4 *The Message Remix* - Eugene H. Peterson
"Over a period of several hundred years, the Hebrew people gave birth to an extraordinary number of prophets - men and women distinguished by the power and skill with which they presented the reality of God. They delivered God's commands and promises and living presence to communities and nations who had been living on god-fantasies and god-lies." p.961

"We don't read very many pages into the Prophets before realizing that there was nothing easygoing about them. Prophets were not popular figures." p.961

"Prophets make it impossible to evade God or make detours around God." p.963

5 *The Prophets* - Abraham J. Heschel
"The prophet is a man who feels fiercely. God has thrust a burden upon his soul." p.5

"The prophet's use of emotional and imaginative language, concrete in diction, rhythmical in movement, artistic in form, marks his style as poetic." p.7

"The prophet seldom tells a story, but casts events." p.8

Plato felt as if "the creative process of the poet resembles or actually is a state of madness." p.499

6 *Between God and Man* - Abraham J. Heschel
"Our quest for God is a return to God; our thinking of Him is a recall." p.71

7 *Between God and Man* - Abraham J. Heschel
"This is at the core of all Biblical thoughts: God is not a being detached from man to be sought after, but a power that seeks, pursues and calls upon man." p.78

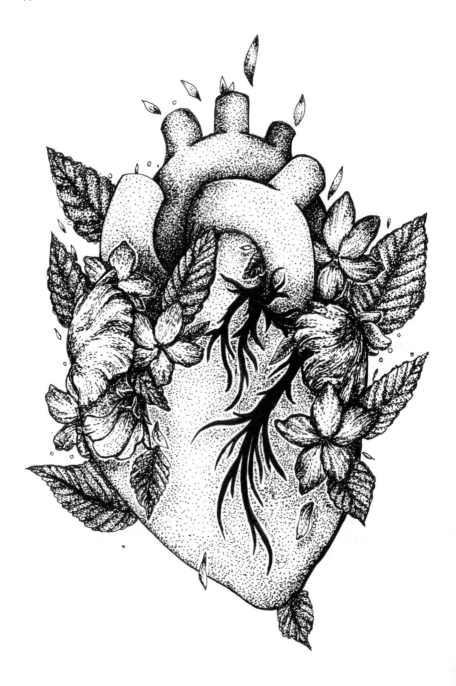

IMAGE 3
HEART

In the *Torah* (Law), God pointed his finger toward something.
Through the *Nevi'im* (Prophets), God demonstrated the work of his hand. The Law and the Prophets brought promise and hope, but no fulfillment.
And when hope is not fulfilled, it's hard.

What do you do with unfulfilled hope?

Generation after generation had gone by with only whispers and prophecies of God's coming Messiah. And after generations of *nothing*, the people created *something.* [1]

Because when people wait too long without seeing a promise fulfilled, they inevitably respond with *something.*

The Writings.
Made up of eleven books (depending on how you categorize the sections of the Bible) of poetry and wisdom, The Writings (*Ketuvim* in Hebrew) make up the final section of the Hebrew Scriptures.

They are a blend of despair and desperate eagerness, a pouring out of trust, anger, disappointment, hope - they are a display of the heart. [2]

The Writings are...*art.*

In total, there are three sections of the Hebrew Scriptures (what we call the Old Testament) and these three sections are what give the Hebrew Scriptures their other name: The Tanakh.

It's an acronym of sorts. The T.N.K.
Torah. Nevi'im. Ketuvim.
The Law. The Prophets. The Writings.

The *Torah* **(finger)** pointed the Way.
The Nevi'im **(hand)** reminded of the Truth.
The *Ketuvim* **(heart)** reflected the Life.

And so the *Tanakh* is sometimes referred to as The Way, The Truth, and The Life.

Though the Scriptures were eventually written down, the average Hebrew family did not have a copy of the Scriptures in their home. This was an oral culture that memorized Scripture in order to pass it down from generation to generation. Therefore, communities often sang in order to remember. Hebrew words have music-style accents and were often meant to be sung. In many ways, the Hebrew language is both musical and poetic. [3]

I remember learning about poetry as a child, with the end of every line having to rhyme. As I got older, I learned that lines don't have to rhyme in order for a poem to...be a poem.

In ancient Hebrew poetry, rhyming was of no cocern. The writers focused on what is now called *parallelism*.
It wasn't about rhyming the sound of something.
It was about paralleling the theme of something.

Here's an example:
"Your word is a **lamp** for my **feet**
a **light** on my **path**."
[Psalm 119.105]

Lamp is paralleled with *Light*.
Feet is paralleled with *Path*.

(Your word lights where I'm walking. And so I'm going to say it twice because it reinforces the point and makes it more memorable.)

It wasn't about rhyming the *sound*. It was written to create memorable parallels. **Because art carries ideas.** This artistic writing approach captures a spectacular range of emotion and thought and represents approximately 75% of the Bible.

Here are some examples of the Writings:

Psalms means *praises*. These poetic songs displayed a range of emotion and thought as it relates to God: Doubt. Fear. Joy. Expectation. Confusion. Anger. Faith and feelings, it seems, are interconnected. [4]

In Proverbs, Solomon wrote ethical instructions in the form of parables, a poetic writing technique to describe the living out of faith.

Job is a story about how people respond to suffering.

Ecclesiastes is written from the perspective of a teacher in the last season of life (sometimes referred to as the Autumn Teacher). It's as if the teacher (commonly thought to be Solomon) is saying: *I'm in the final season of my life, and I have something to say.*

Lamentations is a book of complaining. In Hebrew, lament means *how*. When something bad happens, someone might say *how* could this happen?

Song of Solomon (sometimes call Song of Songs) is the poetry of intimacy.

Some things only make sense in our hearts if we *say* them artistically.
It could've been said directly, but why not write a poem about it?

"Come away, my beloved, and be like a young stag on the spice-laden mountains."
[Song of Solomon 8]

Have you ever painted? Have you every strummed a guitar? Have you ever put your fingers on a piano? Somehow, these expressions say what we can't say. We are designed that way.

We have a wonderful ability to say things that are beyond words.
We create visible representations of how we feel.
Like God did in *the beginning*.
Art is our attempt to make the invisible visible.

The *Ketuvim* covers a spectrum of human emotion.
The Writings are *real*, inviting you to be real.
If The Prophets expressed the emotions of God
toward people, The Writings expressed the emotions
of people toward God.

"How long LORD? Will you forget me forever?"
[Psalm 13]

How would you describe the **strongest** human
emotions? I surveyed people with this question, and
here are some of the answers:

Sadness. Embarrassment. Disgust. Contempt.
Hate. Worthlessness. Bitterness. Loneliness.

Doesn't it seem that our negative emotions are often
stronger than our positive ones? Do you know what
I mean? Sometimes positive words like Peace can
seem generic in comparison to the strength of a
word like *Loneliness*.

I have a theory about this:

**Negative emotions often feel stronger because
they are temporary.** I think that feelings of
loneliness, sadness, and worthlessness can feel
overwhelming because they are packed into a
window of *time*.

As opposed to the other end of the spectrum.

When we have a sense of belonging or community, we are experiencing an eternal emotion, something that will remain after all else is gone. We are feeling the forever-ness of life. [5]

I believe *community* lasts forever, and *loneliness* doesn't.

When we compare loneliness (packed into the temporary) with ongoing community, loneliness can feel stronger. And it's in this tension when humans create some of the best art. Think of the times you've been the most creative.
Was it when everything seemed fine? Or was it in the tension? I think this is why we don't typically like songs that resolve too quickly. If I hear a song like this...

Verse 1: *Everything is fine.*
Verse 2: *Still good.*
Chorus: *Great.*
Bridge: *Still great.*

...I end up thinking, "I didn't like that song. It's too great." And it's funny to think that I wouldn't be as intrigued by a song about things being great.

Why do we often like tension *better*? Why do we like art *more* when someone has agonized over it? I think the answer is the same as the feeling of waiting for the Messiah to come.

The Biblical writings were created in that tension.

What do we do when we feel more than one emotion at the same time?

Do joy, trust, and love seem distant and weak compared to your feelings of doubt and depression?

Sometimes we're afraid to admit this. We are so afraid to admit our weaknesses. Many of us have such an amazing facade, that no one would ever be able to figure us out. And we're afraid that if we ever admit any weakness at all, we'll be cast out. Is that you? Are you afraid that no one is going to listen to you? Or that they won't understand your words? That you'll be an outcast? That they'll think less of you?

I have something to say to you if you feel alone: **Admitting to someone that you are lonely is also admitting to yourself that you are not.**

If you can get the courage to tell someone of your sadness, you are finally admitting to yourself that you might have community. If you're finally willing to tell someone that you don't have anyone, then you're finally admitting to yourself that maybe you *do* have someone.

This is why it's so important for us to **purposefully externalize the tensions that we feel.** When we choose *not* to express our feelings, they *will* manifest somehow. It's inevitable that the invisible will become visible in some way. And if we don't externalize with intentionality, we may externalize in destructive ways.

Let me go a step further.
I think most people doubt their faith.
Myself included.
So let's change the stigma surrounding doubt.
Doubt is not dangerous. It's simply part of the range of human emotion. [6]

For me, as a teacher, studying and teaching on the ways of God, there is a temptation for me not to acknowledge doubt as one my realities. I could be afraid that you would think less of me. By simply stating, "I have doubts. I have never seen God..." the power of my fear is diffused. Instead of living in my own isolated world and thinking that I could never admit that, I choose to externalize it with intentionality.

God knows our limitations. He knows that we can't see the invisible. And I believe that God is so loving, that when we believe in things we've never seen, he's really proud of us. And when we admit doubt, I think he's really proud of us. If you struggle with depression and worthlessness, I think God is proud of you just for getting out of bed.

I think God's proud of you and is with you. God is in the tension with you. You can choose to do things that are hard, because you're not alone in this feeling, even when it seems like you are.

"God sets the lonely in families,
he leads out the prisoners with singing."
[Psalm 68.6]
(See the parallel poetry, by the way?)

If you feel lonely, and sing it out loud, something within you might connect to that same feeling in someone else.

When we admit something *with* others, it's actually a form of communal faith. And there's a word for this in the Bible: it's the word **confess**. It means *to say with or agree with*.

May you realize how lonely you *aren't*. May you begin to believe in the eternal things over the temporary things. If you are willing to externalize the tension intentionally, and even artistically, you have a lot to offer the rest of us.

Some of the best art ever made came out of difficult circumstances.

"Why, my soul, are you downcast? Why so disturbed within me?
Put your hope in God, for I will yet praise him, my Savior and my God."
[Psalm 42.5]

Don't quit. Don't give up on yourself. Don't give up on God.
Blast those favorite songs that express the tension.
Paint. Write. Cry. Shout. Tell the world through art.
But don't give up.
Your temporary feeling of loneliness is not stronger than the power of ongoing community.

There is a rabbinic concept called **kavanah**, which means *direction, intention,* or *devotion.* The idea is to choose to set the direction of your heart toward God. [7]

It is a good thing to know the direction of your own heart. [8]

If you are curious. If you struggle. If you doubt. It means that you are attempting faith. You are *attempting* to see what you can't quite see. [9]

You can question God...
even as you set your heart in the direction that God is pointing...
even if you **still** don't know where that is. [10]

IMAGE 3 NOTES

1 *The Gifts of the Jews* - Thomas Cahill.
Hebrew literature was born in Babylon.
"In three generations the House of David went from exaltation among the nations to unrivaled property to the disaster of a rump state, the Kingdom of Judah. But in that brief time, Hebrew literature was born." p.208

2 *Praying Like the Jew, Jesus* - Timothy P. Jones
"From the beginning, every human heart has craved infinite delight. A dark hungry void gnaws at every human being's innermost self." p.29

3 *Abraham* - Bruce Feiler
The narrative among the Israelite people was an oral narrative for generations. In order to ensure that more and more of the Israelites knew the narrative, "scribes began to write down the story in a comprehensive way." p.120

The Israelites set about codifying their Book, gathering and recording all the oral stories, and making them available to the population. "The invention in the third century B.C.E. of parchment - cheap, processed animal skins used in place of papyrus - helped." p.121
Before that, the only material available was papyrus, which was a rare plant found only in Egypt.

4 Go to YouTube and watch Bono & Eugene Peterson | THE PSALMS.
Peterson:
"The Psalms are not pretty. They're not nice."

"We need to find a way to cuss without cussing."
"We have to have some way, in context, to tell people how mad we are."
Bono:
"These are people who are vulnerable to God."
"Having feelings is perfectly normal. Let them out."

5 *Listening to the Language of the Bible* - Lois Tverberg with Bruce Okkema
The Western mind thinks that knowledge of God "means to prove God's existence and establish a theological model to explain God's nature. But the Hebrew view is that 'knowledge of God' is having a life in relationship with him." p.5

6 *What is the Bible?* - Rob Bell
"The Bible is a book about what it means to be human....The Bible is filled with people wrestling and struggling and doubting and shouting and arguing with this idea that there even is a god, let alone some sort of divine being who is on our side." p.4

7 *Listening to the Language of the Bible* - Lois Tverberg with Bruce Okkema
Read Chapter 38 for a great discussion about the concept of *kavanah*.

8 *Heart* - Sleeping At Last   (Lyrics)
Ryan O'Neal is a singer-songwriter responsible for the music of Sleeping At Last. I dare you to look up the song *Heart* by Sleeping at Last (with the lyrics) and sing it to yourself.
"What if we could risk
Everything we have
And just let our walls cave in..."

9 *Dangerous Wonder* - Michael Yaconelli
"Curiosity is the unknown fruit of the Spirit, the stealthy expression of God's presence." p.39

10 *Learning to Walk in the Dark* - Barbara Brown Taylor
"Did I have enough faith to explore the dark instead of using faith to bar all my doors? How much more was in store for me if I could learn to walk in the dark?" p.9

PRE / FACE

The end of the Hebrew Scriptures.
(The Torah, The Neviim, The Ketuvim)
Old Testament, over.

400 years of silence. No Scripture recorded. No
prophets to bring the word of God. No promises. No
promises fulfilled.

One generation after another waited.

But the Messiah did not come.

Can you identify with this feeling?

Consider writing your own waiting responses in this space.
[No Rules. Just Open Space.]

"Wait for the Lord;
be strong, and let your heart take courage; wait for
the Lord!"
[Psalm 27.14 ESV]

"But as for me, I will look to the Lord;
I will wait for the God of my salvation."
[Micah 7.7 ESV]

"For God alone, O my soul, wait in silence,
for my hope is from him."
[Psalm 62.5 ESV]

IMAGE 4
FACE

400 years of silence
(no prophecies, no heroes, no Scriptures written).

Greek Hellenization had forcefully spread through that part of the world. And by the first century C.E., the Roman Empire had taken over. Judaism in Israel looked very different than in the times of the Old Testament. Israel had a falsely appointed king (Herod), and although the Jewish people were permitted to worship in their homeland, it was a politically and spiritually disjointed time. [1]

Although artistic expressions of faith existed, hope without restoration would eventually lead to hopelessness. Instead of the hope of a united group of people desperately waiting for the Messiah to come and fix everything, the people became a very *disconnected* group. They attempted to figure things out in their *own* way.

Maybe they could fix everything *themselves*.

This is the cultural context of the Gospels (Matthew, Mark, Luke, John).
The beginning of the New Testament. [2]

Different responses emerged. [3]

There were the **Zealots**. The Zealots grabbed their swords and attempted to overthrow governments. Thus, they were attempting to accomplish what they *themselves* hoped and expected from a promised Messiah that didn't seem to be arriving any time soon.

There were **Tax Collectors.** These were Jewish people taking taxes from their Jewish sisters and brothers on behalf of the Roman government (and getting to keep some for themselves). They were considered the sell-outs of their time.

There were **Pharisees**. Pharisees tried to preserve truth. They held to the truth of the *Tanakh* (Hebrew Scriptures/Old Testament) when few others remembered to do so. Pharisees believed a resurrection would occur and that the dead would be raised to life. They were the ones who tried to preserve the Scriptures. But they went too far. They made rules based on the rules. And rules based on the rules that were based on the rules. These extra rules were considered to be *fences around Torah*. God had pointed to the best possible way to go through the *Torah*. But the Pharisees (and others) created *more* rules in order to try to make sure people couldn't even come *close* to accidentally going the wrong way.

There were **Sadducees.** Sadducees only accepted the written *Torah* (Law). They did not embrace the *Nevi'im* (Prophets), the *Ketuvim* (Writings), or any additional oral traditions of Judaism. Sadducees were known for *not* believing that resurrection was possible. They were part of the religious *and* political leadership in Israel, as well as having a political relationship with the Roman government.

There were the **Essenes**. The Essenes lived in the wilderness by themselves because they didn't want to blend in with the Roman culture. They didn't want to be tempted to disobey God's commands, or even accidentally disobey God's commands because of getting swept up into a Roman-influenced lifestyle. The Essene people were extreme and intense. They tried to preserve the truth *without* making more laws to enforce on people. They simply did not want to be polluted by the world.

And there were **Rabbis**. The rabbis were the teachers, the sages. They preserved truths, not by enforcing laws, but by passing down truths to the next generation with their teachings.

Every one of these groups attempted to preserve Jewish culture. Each group tried to figure out Israel's future. Each group struggled in the tension of God's seemingly unfulfilled promises.

And to make things more complicated, there were... reports from shepherds.

And more reports, from intriguing, traveling non-Jewish mystics, who somehow, through prophecy and astrology, claimed that they figured out that the promised Messiah of Israel (and hopefully of the whole world) had been born.

Only a small handful of people were aware of the significance of this baby boy from an unimpressive small town in an unimpressive region of Israel.

It was a *virgin* that conceived and gave birth to this baby, which was spoken of by the prophets. The baby was born in the *place* and in the manner in which the prophets foretold. And the baby grew up. Healthy, in so many ways.

At the age of 12 years old, he began to impress. Teachers in the temple courts were in awe that anyone, let alone a 12-year-old, could understand and discuss theological ideas in the manner that he did.v

So, people may have wondered if he was The One.

But nothing (in particular) happened.

Some must have stayed curious.

Was this more empty hope?
Another chance of restoration, but with no permanent result?

Fast forward about 18 years. An Essene named John, on the outskirts of society, began making a considerable claim. He claimed that God's kingdom had come *near*. [Read Luke 2 and Matthew 3] **4**

He quoted the prophet Isaiah:
"A voice of one calling in the wilderness, 'Prepare the way for the Lord, make straight paths for him. Every valley shall be filled in, every mountain and hill made low. The crooked roads shall become straight, the rough ways smooth. And all people will see God's salvation.'"
[Luke 3.4-6. From Isaiah 40.3-5]

The Essene in the wilderness, John, was functioning as a prophet while quoting a prophet: *"Prepare the way for the Lord."*

What did he mean? Did he mean what the people listening *thought* he meant? Was John referring to the *almostness* of **God with us?**

The finger had pointed.
The hand had reminded.
The heart had cried out.
Will everything be made right? Will everyone see God's *salvation*?
Could it be?

In a small region, near the Sea of Galilee, nowhere near where the religious or political leaders were...the baby that was born of a virgin, who had impressed with his knowledge at age 12, turned 30. He had become a brand new rabbi. (In first-century rabbinic training, a young man had to reach the age of 30 in order to be eligible to become a rabbi.)

In his new rabbinical role, this young rabbi was handed one of the scrolls to read aloud in a synagogue service.

It was finally his turn to read.

Culturally, this would have been considered the beginning of his public rabbinic ministry.

"He stood up to read, and the scroll of the prophet Isaiah was handed to him. Unrolling it, he found the place where it is written:
'The Spirit of the Lord is on me, because he has anointed me to proclaim good news to the poor. He has sent me to proclaim freedom for the prisoners and recovery of sight for the blind, to set the oppressed free, to proclaim the year of the Lord's favor.'" [Luke 4.16-19]

A beautiful sentiment, right?

What an honor to be given the opportunity to read a hopeful prophecy regarding the long-awaited Anointed Messiah.

"Then he rolled up the scroll, gave it back to the attendant and sat down. The eyes of everyone in the synagogue were fastened on him."
[Luke 4.20]

Wait. What?

Ok...He rolled up the scroll...got it.

He gave it back to the attendant...yep.

He sat back down...right.

But why were the eyes of everyone in the synagogue fastened on him?

Well, part of the answer is quite simple, culturally speaking. He was a rabbi. Rabbis stood to read the Scripture and then sat down to teach. So when a rabbi sat down, it was time to start teaching. In some ways, this was a visual representation of the order of importance. Standing for the reading of the Scriptures, which were considered *above* the teachings of man. Sitting to hear man's commentary because it was supplemental, of lower value.

Practically speaking, the people in the synagogue were simply waiting to hear a rabbi teach about what was just read. The eyes of everyone in the synagogue were fastened on him.

But there was another nuance to this moment. He was a *new* rabbi. This new rabbi was already considered to be an amazing teacher. He had been proving himself for years, and they were excited to hear what he had to say.

And there was another significant layer. His early listeners didn't really know who he fully was...yet. They were impressed by his teachings, but unsure or unaware of the magnitude of what was about to happen.

They didn't yet know that he wasn't just a brand new rabbi;
he was a brand new *kind* of rabbi.

"He began by saying to them,
'Today this scripture is fulfilled in your hearing.'"
[Luke 4.21]

Some responded with, "Isn't this Joseph's son?" The sentiment is basically: *Wait. What just happened here?*

Although they had just heard a passionate reminder from the scroll of an ancient prophecy regarding how the Messiah would come and restore things, many hearts may not have been hopeful. These were religious people, who in some ways had all but given up on the Messiah coming.

Apparently, it's possible to believe something is true, but not always be searching for its deepest lessons. It's possible to believe something and yet not *actively* put hope in it.

At most, they would have expected him to sit down and teach, and then they would say that it was *really* good. They would say that they had themselves such a great new rabbi.

But something else was going on, and many of them might not have *really* been paying attention.

What was this new rabbi claiming?
Good teaching is one thing. But claiming that an ancient prophecy had just been fulfilled in their hearing...well, that's something else entirely.

It was as if he were implying that his brief commentary was *not* of a lower status than the Scripture he had just read. He, in essence (and seemingly out of nowhere), claimed:
I AM THE MESSIAH. [5]

Sure, rumors had spread about his being someone special. There was talk that his mother, Mary, had been a virgin when she conceived him, but nothing had come of it in the last 30 years. He was a grown man already. He was a carpenter and had become a great teacher. But he hadn't done anything to save Israel. He hadn't seemingly done anything to even *begin* the process of restoring all things.

Nothing special seemed to be happening.

Hadn't they gone through this before? For hundreds of years, wasn't it always the same cycle of hope, then destruction?

Weren't they just going to be let down again?

This new rabbi's name: **Yeshua of Nazareth.**

Yeshua is a Hebrew and Aramaic name (the primary languages of the Hebrew people).

When the name *Yeshua* was transferred into Greek (the predominant language of the New Testament), the name was *transliterated*. This means that instead of the *meaning* of the word being *translated*, they simply used Greek letters to transfer the *sound* of the name. The name *Yeshua* was *transliterated* into Greek as *Iesous* (sounds sort of like *Yay-soos*). And then, the Greek sound *Iesous* was *transliterated* into English as **Jesus**. If we were to transfer the sounds of the name *Yeshua* into English, we would call him *Joshua*. Remember Joshua? He was the one who brought the people farther than Moses could. [6]

Remember the *meaning* of the name *Yeshua*? **God is salvation.**

And while the name *Yeshua/Jesus* was not a name unique to this young rabbi from Nazareth, *he* was the one claiming that the prophecy was being fulfilled at that moment in the synagogue.

There may have been people in that little synagogue thinking:
Does he mean what I think he means?
And even though the people of his village thought he was a great teacher, they just couldn't believe this.

Some even wanted to have him killed for his claim. As Jesus continued his rabbinic teaching role while traveling around the region (and eventually throughout the nation), he was simultaneously somewhat secretive about his identity, and outright bold in his claims.

In one of his first and most famous teaching moments (sometimes referred to as the *Sermon on the Mount*), Jesus *sat* down on the mountainside, near the Sea of Galilee. He was no longer in his hometown but was teaching in a larger nearby area. He made this claim:

"Do not think that I have come to abolish the Law or the Prophets;
I have not come to abolish them but to fulfill them."
[Matthew 5.17]

Abolish (in the Greek) means to *pour out*.
And *fulfill* means *to overflow*.

Imagine a glass half full (or half empty, depending on your personality). The claim of Jesus was that he had not come to pour out the Scriptures, but to have them overflow. In other words, he had come to bring a full understanding and completeness to them. [7]

In a conversation about life and love and worship, someone once said to him:
"I know that Messiah is coming.
When he comes, he will explain everything to us."
And Jesus replied with:
"I, the one speaking to you - I am he."

[Read John 4]

Later, Jesus told his followers:
"I am the way and the truth and the life." [John 14.6]
Remember that this culture had nicknamed the
Law, Prophets, and Writings
the Way, the Truth, and the Life.

*This was a claim to be even **more** than the promised
Messiah.* This was a claim to *be* the source, essence,
and purpose of the Law, Prophets, and Writings.

**He was claiming to be the finger that was
pointing, the right hand that was reminding, and
the cry to God in the midst of the waiting.**

While in a debate with a religious crowd, Jesus said
to them:
"Your father Abraham rejoiced at the thought of
seeing my day;
he saw it and was glad."
They replied with:
"You are not yet fifty years old, and you have seen
Abraham!"
His reply: "Before Abraham was born, I am."
[Read John 8] [8]

Think about that claim, the claim that he not only
knew things from long ago but was already in existence long ago. Not only was Jesus claiming to have
been alive before the time of Abraham, but he was
also declaring it with a two-word phrase, which in
this culture was the strongest of claims.

Jesus' words were a reference to the Name of God:
I am who I am.
[Read Exodus 3]

Jesus added a major layer to what John had said

about the kingdom. John had said that the kingdom of God was *near*. Jesus said: "The kingdom of God is in your midst." [Luke 17.21]

He was saying that the kingdom of God was no longer just an expectation. No more waiting. Not far off. And not just near, but *here*. [9]

In a culture of Pharisees and Sadducees arguing over politics and religion, struggling over power, and debating over whether the resurrection from the dead was possible, Jesus said: "I am the resurrection." [John 11.25]
Jesus didn't just vote for the resurrection side; he claimed to be the resurrection itself.

Many generations before this, in the wilderness, God had provided bread for the wandering Israelites. That bread was called *manna,* which means *what is it?* When the bread came down from heaven, they said, "What is it?" So they named it *"what is it?"*

So. What is it?
Well, Rabbi Jesus said:
"I am the bread that came down from heaven." [John 6.41]
When the Israelites were waiting in the wilderness, and finally saw something that was tangible for faith, it was him?

That's what Jesus was saying. Long ago when God's people wandered in the wilderness and picked up the bread from the ground - It was *Yeshua*. God is salvation. God is with us.

And if he was in the wilderness in the form of bread from heaven, then *Yeshua* existed before his own birth.

Yeshua existed *before* the baby was born in Bethlehem.

God has been with us the whole time.

The Messiah had come,
and
was here all along.

"In the beginning was the Word, and the Word was with God, and the Word was God. He was with God in the beginning. Through him all things were made; without him nothing was made that has been made."
[John 1.1-3]

This whole time, we've been waiting *for* him. Meanwhile, everything was made *through* him.

The invisible One reveals his visibleness through the visible aspect of his invisibility. He demonstrates that which seemingly cannot be demonstrated.

"The Word became flesh and made his dwelling among us. We have seen his glory, the glory of the one and only Son, who came from the Father, full of grace and truth."
[John 1.14]

The gospel in one short sentiment: The Word became flesh and made his dwelling among us.

God is not a distant God. He became visible, revealed his very nature, and gave people the gift of himself in

Christ Jesus. (The word *Christ* comes from the Greek *Christos,* meaning Messiah). [10]

Somehow, in Jesus, we are able to see the face of God.

"For God, who said, 'Let light shine out of darkness,' made his light shine in our hearts to give us the light of the knowledge of God's glory displayed in the face of Christ."
[2 Corinthians 4.6]

Despite doing no wrong, Jesus died on a cross (a punishment reserved by Romans for criminals).

Jesus overcame death through his resurrection. (Of course he would rise from the dead. He *is* resurrection.)

Sin, death, darkness, and brokenness are not the *point* of the story. The finger was never pointing in accusation against you.

God was pointing to himself the whole time. [11]
How could there be anywhere better to go than to him? Everything was made by him. Everything was made for him. Everything was made through him.

The finger was always pointing to and *through* Jesus.

IMAGE 4 NOTES

1 *The Jews in the Time of Jesus* - Stephen Wylen
"One can never know Jesus' Judaism only from reading the Hebrew scriptures." p.8

2 *The Voice New Testament* - Ecclesia Bible Society
"The phrase 'New Testament' goes back to the prophet Jeremiah. About 600 years before Jesus performed His first miracle, the prophet received a message from the Eternal One. In that oracle, he said that a day will come when God establishes a new covenant with His people. (Jeremiah 31.31-34)" p. xix

3 Recommended Reading: *Desire of Everlasting Hills: The World Before and After Jesus* - Thomas Cahill

4 *The Divine Conspiracy* - Dallas Willard
Willard writes about the kingdom as "a realm that is uniquely our own, where our choice determines what happens...Our kingdom is simply *the range of our effective will.*" p.21

"God's own 'kingdom,' or 'rule,' is the range of his effective will....The person of God himself and the action of his will are the organizing principles of his kingdom, but everything that obeys those principles, whether by nature or by choice, is *within* his kingdom." p.25

5 "The people were amazed at his teaching, because he taught them as one who had authority, not as the teachers of the law." [Mark 1.22]

This sort of authority is described in the book *Come with Me: Lessons Learned on our walk through Israel.*

Many teachers knew scriptures, "but were limited to the teachings of their communities." However, rarely someone would come along with something they called "s'mikeh." *S'mikeh* meant authority, and rabbis with *s'mikeh* had the right to teach NEW things, not just the traditions of their community. They were something altogether different.
-From Gwen Hanna p.120

6 *The Jews in the Time of Jesus* - Stephen M. Wylen Jesus would most likely have spoken to the Jewish community primarily in Aramaic, read the scriptures primarily in Hebrew, and spoken Greek while in the Roman-occupied Greek cities. The primary language of Israel in the first century was Greek because of the Hellenization process. p.33

The Jews spoke Aramaic, a language they picked up when Babylon took over that part of the world. p.36

"Jesus, the Galilean Jew, spoke the Aramaic language. He preached in Aramaic. His teachings, his prayers, his religious terminology, all spoke directly to the relatively non-Hellenized Jews of the land of Israel." p.47

7 *To Know as We are Known: Education as a Spiritual Journey* - Parker J. Palmer
"Hidden inside our words, buried at the very roots, are ancient word pictures which often tell us more than contemporary usage reveals." p.22

8 *Evolution of the Word* - Marcus J. Borg
"Jesus was an itinerant teacher whose most characteristic forms of speech were striking short sayings, called 'aphorisms,' and short stories, called 'parables.' The use of memorable aphorisms and parables is a brilliant and necessary strategy for a teacher in a preliterate and preprint culture." p.13

9 *Kingdom* - United Pursuit (song lyrics)
"I believe in a Kingdom that's much more real than what we see."

10 *Praying Like the Jew, Jesus* - Timothy P. Jones
"God blessed his people by giving them the gift of himself." p.117

"Blessedness is not about receiving things; it is about receiving God." p.20

11 *The Message Remix* - Eugene Peterson
"The arrival of Jesus signaled the beginning of a new era. God entered history in a personal way, and made it unmistakably clear that he is on our side, doing everything possible to save us." p.1425

IMAGE 5
FEET

Doesn't it seem like this would already be the end of the story?
Jesus' resurrection conclusively settled the argument between the Pharisees and Sadducees. Fade to black...roll the credits. Right?

The finger of God was always pointing *to* and *through* Jesus.

Apparently, there is more.

The age-old mystery remained:
What are we walking toward?
Where is this story headed?

Up until this point in history, the hope of the promised Messiah was primarily thought to be for the Israelites (the Jewish people) and their freedom from the oppression of surrounding countries. But the prophets spoke about much, much more. Namely, that the Israelites would be a light to all nations. The prophet Isaiah had said that God would use the Israelites to bring salvation to the very ends of the earth.
[Isaiah 49.6]

After Jesus resurrected, but before he ascended back into the heavens, he echoed this thought and told his original followers that they would be his witnesses not only in Jerusalem but all over the world.
[Acts 1.8]

And so, the earliest Jewish believers in Jesus began to spread the message of hope beyond their own borders. They traveled throughout the known world with the message of the gospel of Jesus and told the Gentiles that they too were invited and included in this good news. (The word *gospel* means *good news*).

As the community of believers grew (numerically and geographically), there were more and more topics that needed clarification. Eventually, most new believers were Gentiles who would not have known the *Torah*, Prophets, and Writings. The early church grew into a group of people around the world who believed in Jesus but did not always know the fullness of what that really meant. They believed that Jesus was the Messiah, but did not fully understand the need for — and the promise of — the Messiah.

It was as if they knew the answer, but didn't know the question.

Letters were written by the original Jewish believers in Jesus and sent to new believers in order to help explain the nuances of the good news, as well as how to share it with the world. These letters were intended to be read out loud, as a community. [1]

Some aspects of these letters were theological in nature (belief about who God is). Other aspects of the letters dealt with morality (how to treat each other). Overall, it could be said that **the letters put words to how theology can be accurately demonstrated in the way believers live.**
Now that the long-awaited Messiah has come, how do we *live*?

Now that Jesus has overcome sin, death, and brokenness, how do we *walk* it out? [2]

When I was 22, I got a flyer in the mail. It was one of those *get-rich-quick* flyers. The system they were selling was $19.95. I hesitantly admit that I bought it. A week later, a VHS tape showed up in the mail. I was excited. I'd just watch a video, do what it said, and I'd be rich. Sounded awesome. In the video, there was a guy giving a seminar, using a flip chart, explaining how to sell the video.
Let me repeat that. The video was of a guy explaining how to sell the video.

Did you catch that? **There was no product.**

I'm afraid that much of the message of Christianity has been reduced to this.

The system:
Step one: Say you believe in Jesus.
Step two: Tell other people to believe in Jesus.
Step three: Why? So they can tell other people to believe in Jesus.

What do we *do* after believing in Jesus? What does believing in Jesus *lead to*? Does it only lead to *convincing* other people to believe in Jesus?

Have we come to a place where we think that convincing someone else to believe what we believe *is* the good news? Are we trying to get people to believe something that we don't even understand ourselves? What are we doing?

The gospel is about reconciliation. It's about the restoration of relationship.

In one of the letters to the Gentile (non-Jewish) believers, Paul (a Jewish believer) said it this way: "For he himself is our peace, who has made the two groups one and has destroyed the barrier, the dividing wall of hostility, by setting aside in his flesh the law with its commands and regulations. His purpose was to create in himself one new humanity out of the two, thus making peace, and in one body to reconcile both of them to God through the cross, by which he put to death their hostility." [Ephesians 2.14-16]

Jesus' followers had to deal with generations of conflict and division between Jews and Gentiles. Due to a long history of political and religious differences (as well as endless wars), there was significant distrust among the two groups. The Jewish people considered the Gentiles to be outside of the promises of God. This led to labeling Gentiles as unclean and sinful. Based on commands from God about maintaining purity, the Jewish people had added rules upon rules (*fences around Torah*) that led to complete separation. Jews didn't touch Gentiles. Didn't approach them. Didn't speak to them. Different races being united in faith was a new idea for both groups, and often quite difficult to navigate. Messiah Jesus had removed the barrier. Now there was one new person in Christ, no more divide between Jew and Gentile. The early followers of Jesus had to learn what that meant.

In another letter to the Gentile believers, the idea of reconciliation seemed to e x p a n d :

"The Son is the image of the invisible God, the firstborn over all creation. For in him all things were created: things in heaven and on earth, visible and invisible, whether thrones or powers or rulers or authorities; all things have been created through him and for him. He is before all things, and in him all things hold together. And he is the head of the body, the church; he is the beginning and the firstborn from among the dead, so that in everything he might have the supremacy. For God was pleased to have all his fullness dwell in him, and through him to **reconcile to himself all things**, whether things on earth or things in heaven, by making peace through his blood, shed on the cross. Once you were alienated from God and were enemies in your minds because of your evil behavior. But now he has reconciled you by Christ's physical body through death to present you holy in his sight, without blemish and free from accusation."
[Colossians 1.15-22]

Jesus, the visible version of the invisible God, was revealed in order to bring everything together.
Heaven and earth. Visible and invisible.
Everything.

The early church was beginning to realize that the implications of reconciliation went far beyond a divide between Jews and Gentiles. There was more reconciliation to come. The story hadn't ended.

In yet another letter, we read:
"We always carry around in our body the death of Jesus, so that the life of Jesus may also be revealed in our body. For we who are alive are always being given over to death for Jesus' sake, so that **his life may also be revealed in our mortal body.**"
[2 Corinthians 4.10,11]

His life revealed in us.
We have a role to play in this story.

"If anyone is in Christ, the new creation has come: The old has gone, the new is here! All this is from God, who reconciled us to himself through Christ and **gave us the ministry of reconciliation**: that God was reconciling the world to himself in Christ, not counting people's sins against them."
[2 Corinthians 5.17-19]

We've been invited into the reconciliation.

The Greek word used here for *reconciliation is katallassō.*
Kata, meaning *toward,* and *allassō,* meaning *exchange for another.*
Therefore, *katallassō* can be translated as *exchange.*
A back and forth movement.

Reconciliation, then, is an exchange of yourself for the other.
It's a movement toward the other. ³

To be invited into reconciliation is therefore very much like the Hebrew idea of faith (*emunah: to move toward*), like when Abraham attempted to count the stars and walked in the direction of what he did not yet see. This is the very essence of the gospel, is it not? God moved toward us in Christ.

God
moved
toward
us.

A letter was written to the Hebrew followers of Jesus. The letter opens with:
"Now **faith** is confidence in what we hope for and **assurance about what we do not see.** This is what the ancients were commended for. By faith we understand that the universe was formed at God's command, so that what is seen was not made out of what was visible."
[Hebrews 11.1-3] ⁴

Moving in faith and moving toward others are so connected, actually, that we are reminded in 1 John 4 that "whoever claims to love God yet hates a brother or sister is a liar. For whoever does not love their brother and sister, whom they have seen, cannot love God, whom they have not seen."

Later in the same letter to the Hebrew believers, encouragement is given:
"Since we are surrounded by such a great cloud of witnesses, let us throw off everything that hinders and the sin that so easily entangles. And **let us run with perseverance** the race marked out for us."
[Hebrews 12.1]

The early believers in Jesus weren't just spreading a message. They were continuing in the tradition of Abraham. They were *moving toward,* by faith. Their feet were moving forward. Their roots were being freed, pulling from the ground, and now they were *running.* [5]

The **finger** *pointed.*
The **hand** *reminded.*
The **heart** *cried.*
The **face** *revealed.*
And then the **feet** *proclaimed.* [6]

Our message is not "You're wrong" or "You need to believe what I believe."
The invitation is "Let's throw off all that weighs us down, and run...together." [7]

It turns out, though, that the completion of this story
isn't about knowing *where we are going,*
but knowing *who we are.* [8]

Which leads us to *the whole thing*...

IMAGE 5 NOTES

1 *Evolution of the Word* - Marcus J. Borg
"Paul did not often refer to what Jesus said and did. He wrote to communities that he had taught in person, and so he would already have told them about Jesus....The purpose of Paul's letters was not to tell people about Jesus, but to stay in touch with his communities and to address issues that had arisen in his absence. They are about applications of Paul's understanding of life 'in Christ' - to particular circumstances." p.11

"During the time of Jesus, written documents were not an effective way to spread a message. Writing, of course, did have a purpose. Letters - like the letters of Paul - were a way of communicating with a community that had somebody who could read the letter aloud to the rest. Gospels were a way of preserving an early Christian community's traditions about Jesus." p.12

2 *Come with Me: Lessons Learned on our walk through Israel*
"Truth is not merely known, it must be lived, understood through experience, felt and deeply appreciated." -Randy Hazenberg p. 39

3 "Jesus didn't give us all the answers, but he gave us himself. So stop trying to give people your answers. And just give them yourself." -John Mark McMillan

4 "Faith restores our humanity, and we start living in the future invisible.

It brings us back to our original intention. Faith restores to us what it means to be human" -Erwin McManus

5 "Forgetting what is behind me and straining forward toward what lies ahead, I keep pursuing the goal in order to win the prize offered by God's upward calling." [Philippians 3.13,14 CJB]

6 "How, then, can they call on the one they have not believed in? And how can they believe in the one of whom they have not heard? And how can they hear without someone preaching to them? And how can anyone preach unless they are sent? As it is written: 'How beautiful are the feet of those who bring good news!'"
[Romans 10.14,15]

"How beautiful on the mountains are the feet of those who bring good news, who proclaim peace, who bring good tidings, who proclaim salvation, who say to Zion, 'Your God reigns!'"
[Isaiah 52:7]

7 "It is not the role of the Church to tell people not to sin and to devise lists. The world perfectly knows what sin is. The world knows what morality is. The world knows what's right. Morality is the world's cup of tea. What the world doesn't know is forgiveness and that's what the world needs to be told." -Robert Farrar Capon

8 "For now we see only a reflection as in a mirror; then we shall see face to face. Now I know in part; then I shall know fully, even as I am fully known."
[1 Corinthians 13.12]

IMAGE 6
BODY

Let's go back to the beginning.

I want to look at *the whole thing* in a different way.

"In the beginning God created the heavens and the earth.
Now the earth was formless and empty,
darkness was over the surface of the deep,
and the Spirit of God was hovering over the waters."
[Genesis 1.1,2]

Darkness was over the surface.

In the Hebrew language, **darkness** is associated with **blindness**.

The word **surface** (*paniym* in Hebrew) means **face**.

So the very beginning of the narrative is:

**In the beginning,
God created the heavens and the earth...**
and the face couldn't be seen.

The story starts with an unseen face. [1]
Then...
"God said, 'Let there be light,' and there was light."
[Genesis 1.3]

There it is.
The whole thing was *pre/faced* in the beginning.

Darkness, then light.
Unseen, then seen.
Invisible, then visible.

From the voice of the invisible came the visible. **God did not create from nothing, but from himself.** God said *let there be light*, and we later find out that *God is light* [1 John 1.5]. God *is* the very thing that he spoke. Creation is made *of* God. He began with light, and then created water and sky and ground, plants and animals and everything else. Well, almost.

Finally, a man and a woman were made in the image of God.
The invisible God had an image, a likeness that was masculine and feminine.

The Hebrew word for *image* is *tselem,* meaning *resemblance.*

The Hebrew word *adam* was used to describe *humanity.*
And this word comes from the word *adama*, meaning *earth.*
God formed humanity from the dust of the earth. From the dirt.

We are dirt-people, and we look like God.

We are made of the visible stuff that came from the

voice of the invisible God. God made *it* then made *us* from it. Humanity is not just made *in* the image of God, but made *of* the image of God. [2]

This is the beginning of *our* story. It's not bad being made of the dirt. After humanity was formed, God said that it was *very good*.

The man and the woman didn't walk in that truth very well.

Disobedience and brokenness entered the story very, very quickly. They didn't stay *grounded* in their true identity. They disobeyed their Creator, demonstrating that they didn't completely trust him. Then they covered their bodies, no longer able to see each other for who they were initially made to be.

And thus, they were sentenced to return to the earth, back to the dirt, in death. The consequences of disobedience are costly, and not to be taken lightly. [3]

This happened so quickly, in fact, that brokenness is often the primary focus of the human narrative. But let's remember that the initial act of God in *our* part of the story was creating the man and woman in his image.

Our disobedience doesn't define us. Our likeness does.

The root of the human narrative is not brokenness, but wholeness. [4]

From the beginning, God had a purpose, that we would reflect his wholeness.

"I make known the end from the beginning, from ancient times,
what is still to come. I say, 'My purpose will stand.'"
[Isaiah 46.10]

Do you believe that God's purpose will stand? Or do you think your brokenness is stronger? [5]

The story began with God making man and woman in his image, and even though we may *think* that we somehow ruined it, he will finish His task.
God will complete us fully into his image.

This is God's story to tell, and in his story of *us*, we are made whole. [6]
Our disobedience hasn't derailed his narrative.
From the beginning, the story has always been about this very thing.

God spoke light when darkness hovered over the surface of the deep, and God speaks light into the dark places of our hearts.

Remember?
"For God, who said, 'Let light shine out of darkness,' made his light shine in our hearts to give us the light of the knowledge of God's glory displayed in the face of Christ."
[2 Corinthians 4.6]

In and through Christ, not only does God's light

shine in our darkness,
we are told that *we* shine in the darkness of the world.

"You will shine like stars in the sky."
[Philippians 2.15] [7]

Remember that long ago, Abraham was invited to count the stars in order to understand how big his family would be. He was invited to have faith and move toward the unknown.

And now, here we are. It turns out that he was moving toward all of us. We are like the stars in the sky. We're joined to Abraham as his descendants of faith - **it's the direction of our hearts that connect us**. It's time for us to believe who we really are. [8]

There is a well-known idiom that seems to have originated in the Bible:
The apple of your eye (found in Deuteronomy 32.10 and Psalm 17.8).
Humanity is considered to be the *apple of God's eye*. This is typically thought to mean that we are cherished above all others. But it's an idiom. So let's take a closer *look*.

Let's start with *apple*.
In the Hebrew, the word translated as *apple* is *iyshown*. The literal translation is *dark part* or *pupil*. It's the black, center part of the human eye, which is the part that lets the light in, by the way. It's through the center of the darkness that the light enters.
Iyshown is thought to be related to the word *iysh*, meaning *man*.

Now, *eye*.
The Hebrew word is *ayin*. It means...well...*eye*.
It can also mean *appearance or resemblance*.
There it is again. *Resemblance*.

Have you ever noticed that when you look into someone's eyes, you can see your own reflection in their pupils,
a little image of yourself?

The apple of my eye can be literally translated into *the little man in my eye*.

We are the *little man in the eye of God*. We are made in God's image, after all.
As we look into the face of God through Christ, we see our reflection in his eyes.

––––––

This imagery of face-to-faceness can be traced back to the Hebrew word for *love (aheb)*. *Aheb* means *to long for*, *desire*, *breathe for,* or *breathe with*.
This is an extremely intimate image.
It also has a more primitive, earthy connotation of *being connected to*.
When a seed goes into the soil, it is *connected* with the ground. This connectedness leads to a tree or vine emerging, and eventually, branching out. The ultimate evidence of the connectedness is when a branch bears fruit.

Therefore, *love* is the fruit that is produced and is evidence of the connection.

The first thing (that we know of) that God said to

humanity...
God's first *instruction* to us...
"be fruitful and increase in number." [Genesis 1.28]

We are made to be connected to the dirt.
We are made to be face-to-face with God and with one another.
We are made to love.

Love is the fulfillment of God's instruction. [Romans 13.10]

As it turns out...Love is the *point* of *The Whole Thing*.

In 1 John 4, we learn that "God is love....No one has ever seen God; but if we love one another, God lives in us, and his love is made **complete in us.**"

Love is deeply connected with the dirt. In love, Christ identified with our death by dying and going into the earth. And he overcame death by rising from the dead. He overcame the idea of death being considered bad.

God wants us to be like the Messiah, to know what it is to die for another. [9]
It's in the dying that we will believe that what Christ says about himself is true.
He *is* the resurrection. And like him, we will also resurrect, because we are made to be like him, thus fulfilling the ultimate purpose for which we were made. [10]

The burden of death that came from the consequence of disobedience was redeemed in and through Christ. And now humanity's connection with the dirt is an indicator of our potential.

In our bodies and in our hearts, we die and are planted so that we can be transformed into the fullness of what we were always intended for. [11]

But what is planted is not the same thing as what emerges from the ground.

"When you sow, you do not plant the body that will be, but just a seed."
[1 Corinthians 15.37]

What is sown does not come to life unless it dies. That's how it works.
What is alive dies and bears a seed. The seed is put in the ground. And from it comes new life. The idea that we must experience some form of death in order to be raised into a new life isn't that crazy. It's how the whole of creation already works. [12]

"The body that is sown is perishable, it is raised imperishable; it is sown in dishonor, it is raised in glory; it is sown in weakness, it is raised in power; it is sown a natural body, it is raised a spiritual body. If there is a natural body, there is also a spiritual body."
[1 Corinthians 15.42-44]

When you sow, you do not plant the body that will be, but just a seed.
And then something new emerges. [13]

"I consider that our present sufferings are not worth comparing with the glory that will be revealed in us. The creation waits in eager expectation for the

children of God to be revealed. For the creation was subjected to frustration, not by its own choice, but by the will of the one who subjected it, in hope that the creation itself will be liberated from its bondage to decay and brought into the freedom and glory of the children of God."
[Romans 8.18-21]

All of creation is waiting, because something is coming. [14]
And so our part of the story isn't finished yet. [15]
The creation is waiting for this glory to be revealed in us.
Yes. God's **glory**...revealed...**in us**! [16]

Do you understand who *we* are yet?

As God's children, we are his seeds. We will be planted in the dirt, and emerge as the collective body of God through Christ. [17]

God has a *body*.

And it's us. [18]

God *pointed* to and through the face of Jesus,
to the *little man in his eyes*,
to the body of God: our true selves. [19]

We were the last made among the creation. But we forgot who we were, [20]
and the rest of the creation began to decay because of it.
When the glory of God is revealed in us, the rest of creation will also be brought into this glory. When we realize who we are, the rest of creation will be able to realize as well. [21]

"For as in Adam all die, so in Christ all will be made alive." [1 Corinthians 15.22]

This will be a final revealing that everything he created is his body. [22]
We will be the first to be made whole. Then the rest of the creation after us.
And so the last shall be first.
And the first shall be last.

IMAGE 6 NOTES

1 In his hauntingly rich book, *The Solace of Fierce Landscapes*, Belden C. Lane explained that the apophatic tradition is known for "emphasizing the importance of reaching 'beyond' (*apo*) every 'image' (*phasis*) one might use to speak of God." p.62
The apophatic teachers remind us to connect with God beyond the seeing, in the act of unseeing (often in the form of silent, contemplative prayer).

2 "He is not saying that what is seen was created out of nothing. He's saying what is seen, what is visible, what is material, was created out of that which is not visible. There's a difference. See, God didn't create out of nothing. He created out of something that is invisible material."
"You were invisible material."
"You were a dream in the mind of God."
-Erwin McManus

3 *To Know as We are Known* - Parker J. Palmer
"Adam and Eve were driven from the Garden because of the *kind* of knowledge they reached for - a knowledge that distrusted and excluded God.... They failed to honor the fact that God knew them first, knew them in their limits as well as their potentials." p.25

4 *Wholeheartedness* - Chuck DeGroat
"*Wholeness is our birthright*. Oneness is our most original state of being. And although our experience of division makes us feel as if we're being pulled in a thousand different directions, we can always -

always - return to our center. Though we may be fractured images of God, we're nonetheless images, restored and matured as we take the time to reflect on our lives, to make sense of our stories, and to experience the oneness for which we've been made." p.108-109

5 *Wholeheartedness* - Chuck DeGroat
"*I'm not enough*. This isn't an accusation that arises just in our minds. No, we feel it in our bodies: it burns in our chest. It's palpable. And the accusation is born of shame, perhaps the most violating inner stranger of them all." p.15

6 *Everything Belongs* - Richard Rohr
"Spirituality is about seeing. It's not about earning or achieving. It's about relationship rather than results or requirements. Once you see, the rest follows. You don't need to push the river, because you are in it." p.31
"There's no answer, no problem-solving, simply awareness. You cannot *not* live in the presence of God." p.51

7 *Wholeheartedness* - Chuck DeGroat
"God takes up residence. The Inner Light conquers our darkness, and cannot be extinguished. And recognition of this Inner Light is the first sacramental step on the road to wholeness and wholeheartedness." p.81

8 *The Interior Castle* - St. Teresa of Avila
"For the most part, all our trials and disturbances come from our *not* understanding ourselves." (IV, 1, 9)

9 "Do not depend on the hope of results. In the end, it is the reality of personal relationships that saves everything." - Thomas Merton

10 *Desire of Everlasting Hills* - Thomas Cahill
"And did not all descend, because of [Adam's] disobedience, to the bent and broken world...the world of disease, death, and disharmony, the world that we all inhabit? Did not Jesus, by his resurrection, by this startling proof of life beyond death, set this process of decay going in the opposite direction? Did he not, in effect, by his resurrection (and the promise of ours) reinstitute the Creation? Is he not, therefore, the New Adam, and are we not the New Creation?" p.124

11 *The Divine Conspiracy* - Dallas Willard
"Our human life, it turns out, is not destroyed by God's life but is fulfilled in it and in it alone." p.14 (Remember, this is what Jesus said in Matthew 5.17. He didn't come to abolish, but fulfill.)

12 "Paul personifies the Earth, our kin, as groaning for our collective liberation. Humans and creation are joined at the site of the dirt." -Kat Armas (Host of The Protagonistas Podcast)

13 *Generous Orthodoxy* - Brian McLaren
"What we will be is not yet clear to us. What we are becoming is presently only visible as through a glass darkly. As we see the glorious image of God in the face of Christ, as we lean toward that image that beckons us forward, as we identify it as our true destiny and the pearl of great price that we seek, we are purified and transformed inwardly, from glory to glory. We constantly emerge from what we were and are into what we can become - not just as individuals, but as participants in the emerging realities of families, communities, cultures, and worlds." p.322

14 *An Altar in the World: A Geography of Faith* - Barbara Brown Taylor. "Whoever you are, you are human. Wherever you are, you live in the world, which is just waiting for you to notice the holiness in it." p.xix

15 *The Gifts of the Jews* - Thomas Cahill "We need not fear God as we fear all other suffering, which burns and maims and kills. For God's fire, though it will perfect us, will not destroy [us]." p.164

16 *Heavenly Father* - Bon Iver (song lyrics) *"I was never sure how much of you I could let in."*

17 "You are the body of Christ. And each one of you is a part of it." [1 Corinthians 12.27]

"The church is not a religious community of worshippers of Christ but is Christ himself who has taken form among people." - Dietrich Bonhoeffer

18 *Three* - Sleeping At Last (song lyrics) "For the first time I see an image of my brokenness Utterly worthy of love... And I finally see myself Through the eyes of no one else... I only want what's real I set aside the highlight reel And leave my greatest failures on display with an asterisk Worthy of love anyway"

19 "We say Jesus is fully human and fully divine, because we believe Jesus is the paradigm of what all reality is. If we don't affirm it in him [Jesus], and we won't affirm it about us, we'll never affirm it about everything. You too are fully human and fully divine. You too, are one with God." - My friend, Danny Prada

20 *Body* - Sleeping at Last (song lyrics)
"There's magic in our bones,
A north star in our soul
That remembers our way home.
God, it's easy to forget
There's magic in all of this."

21 *Wholeheartedness* - Chuck DeGroat
"Where we bring our wholeness, others experience wholeness." p.63

22 *Your God is Too Small* - J.B. Phillips
"Let us fling wide the doors and windows of our minds and make some attempt to appreciate the 'size' of God. He must not be limited to religious matters or even to the 'religious' interpretation of life. He must not be confined to one particular section of time nor must we imagine Him as the local god of this planet or even only of the universe that astronomical survey has so far discovered. It is not, of course, physical size that we are trying to establish in our minds." p.63

"For since the creation of the world God's invisible qualities - his eternal power and divine nature - have been clearly seen, being understood from what has been made." [Romans 1.20]

We don't worship "created things rather than the Creator" (Romans 1.25). We acknowledge that God's invisible qualities are demonstrated through visible things. Thus, creation itself isn't the fullness of the reality of God. Instead, creation is full of the reality of God. God exists in and through and beyond all time and space. Thus, the entire universe is full of the

presence of God.
The infinite displayed as finite. The invisible displayed as visible. Maybe the shape is less important than what's conveyed.

The Body of God: An Ecological Theology - Sallie McFague
What is the body? Is body based on **shape or scope?** The word "body" is a noun, referring to the physical structure of a person or an animal, including the bones, flesh, and organs. It can also mean a large or substantial amount of something; a mass or collection of something.

God is everywhere, but what makes this story so significant is that God's presence "is both the concrete, physical availability of God's presence ('became flesh') and the likeness to ourselves, a human being ('lived among us') that matter." p.160

"The metaphor of the cosmic Christ suggests that the cosmos is moving *toward* salvation and that this salvation is taking place *in* creation. The other dimension is that God's presence in the form or shape of Jesus' paradigmatic ministry is available not just in the years 1-30 C.E. and not just in the church as his mystical body, but everywhere, in the cosmic body of the Christ." p.180

Everything Belongs - Richard Rohr
"He makes visible the hiding place of God. His body is the revelation of the essential mystery. The material world is the hiding place of God....God is perfectly hidden, but once the scales have been taken from our eyes, God is also perfectly revealed and you see the divine image in all material things." p.100

THE WHOLE THING

We began at the start of the story. Now, let's move to the end of it. [1]
In the Bible's final book, Revelation, we see something epic happen. We tend to overuse the word epic. Everything in our culture has become *literally the most amazing thing ever*. But this is, for real, epic.

The writer of the book, John (one of the first followers of Jesus), describes a future shown to him by God. [2]

In Revelation 5, John describes God seated on a throne holding a scroll in his right hand. An angel asks, who is worthy to open the scroll? But no one in heaven or on earth can open and read the scroll.

And John weeps because no one is found worthy.

Then the passage continues.
A lamb from the tribe of Judah comes forward to stand before the throne. This lamb is the one who was slain and triumphed.

He takes the scroll and is able to see inside (like when Jesus opened and read the Isaiah scroll in the Nazareth synagogue). And a new song comes:
"You are worthy to take the scroll and to open its seals, because you were slain, and with your blood you purchased for God persons from every tribe and language and people and nation. You have made them to be a kingdom and priests to serve our God, and they will reign on the earth." [Revelation 5.9,10]

This is the visual we're given of humanity at the close of the story!
It's a humanity that God has perfected into the full image of himself, and the image includes all nations, races, tribes, and languages. All are represented.

But it gets even better. John keeps writing:
"Then I saw 'a new heaven and a new earth,' [a quote from Isaiah 65.17]
for the first heaven and the first earth had passed away,
and there was no longer any sea." [Revelation 21.1]

Instead of the darkness of deep waters covering the face, the new earth has no sea, no surface of the deep. There is nothing blocking the face.

And "there will be no more death" because "the old order of things has passed away." [Revelation 21.4]

It's a long story of newness. New heaven. New earth.
New bodies.
New everything. ³

"I am making everything new!"
[Revelation 21.5]

The end of the story has circled back around to the beginning.

"They will see his face, and his name will be on their foreheads.
There will be no more night. They will not need the light of a lamp or the light of the sun, for the Lord God will give them light."
[Revelation 22.4]

No more darkness. No longer will the face be unseen.
That's how face-to-face you will be -
His Name on your forehead (such beautiful imagery)
as if his face is leaning into your face until they touch. [4]

So this is the story of God and of us.
God is invisible. Right?
Actually, the entire message of the Bible points to
and through the face of Christ, in order for us to see
God AND ourselves.

In Revelation 22.21, the story of the Bible closes with:
"'Yes, I am coming soon.' Amen. Come, Lord Jesus.
The grace of the Lord Jesus be with God's people.
Amen." [5]

May the Lord bless you and keep you.
And may his face turn toward you
and shine on you
and be gracious to you
and give you peace.
[based on Numbers 6.24-26]

May you believe these things
about God.
And may you also believe these things
about yourself.
And about all of us.
And about everything.

THE WHOLE THING NOTES

1 *Sort of Revolution* - FINK - Fin Greenall (song lyrics)
"We've come so far, it feels so real
All this time, that we've waited for it
And who we are, and where we're going to
All this time, preparing for it
Come so far
Come so far
So let me know when we get there, if we get there"

2 *The Message Remix* - Eugene H. Peterson
"The Bible ends with a flourish: vision and son, doom and deliverance, terror and triumph. The rush of color and sound, image and energy, leaves us reeling. But if we persist through the initial confusion and read on, we begin to pick up the rhythms, realize the connections, and find ourselves enlisted as participants." p.1813

3 *The Brothers Karamazov* - Fyodor Dostoyevsky
"Love all of God's creation, the whole and every grain of sand of it. Love every leaf, every ray of God's light. Love the animals, love the plants, love everything. If you love everything, you will perceive the divine mystery of things. Once you perceive it, you will begin to comprehend it better every day. And you will come at last to love the whole world with an all-embracing love." - Book VI, Chapter 3, Section G.

4 "Between God and the soul there is no between." - St. Julian of Norwich

5 *22 (Over Soon)* - Bon Iver (song lyrics)
"There I find you marked in constellation
There isn't ceiling in our garden
And then I draw an ear on you
So I can speak into the silence
It might be over soon"

POINTED

REMINDED

CRIED

REVEALED

PROCLAIMED

COMPLETE

ACKNOWLEDGMENTS

Thank you to my dear friends who took time to help edit this book: Macon Atkinson, Kimberly English, Lucas Kovasckitz, Benjamin Ray, Aaron White.

Thank you Belle, for your creativity and talent in creating the images, cover art, and design efforts. Thank you for listening, for your patience, and your love. You are so good.

Thank you to everyone who believed in me and supported this book with your time, love and resources. In particular, I want to give a special acknowledgment of gratitude for the gracious support from Tim Herdklotz, Matt Matthews, John Page, Steve and Lorrie Presnell, Benjamin Ray, Phil Root, Carol Laney Schenck, Olivia Vanarthos, William J. Vanarthos, and Aaron White.

Thank you Katherine Gunning, for the ongoing creative support, as well as coordinating the book launch.

Thank you Justin Davis and Jonathan Weaver, from helping to narrow down the images that one day over coffee.

Thank you to theHeart staff, leadership, and entire church family. I'm honored to be able to partner together in our amazing mountain town.

Thank you dad, for always believing in me.
Thank you mom, for your support, and for thinking I'm great.

Grey and Violet, thank you for being proud of me. It means more to me than I can put into words. I'm so thankful that I get to be your dad.

Kimberly,
I could not and would not have finished the book without you. I'm in awe of the countless hours you spent editing. Thank you. Your recommendations and suggestions saved the day. I will always remember our conversations.
You show me what God is like.
The last shall be first.

ABOUT
THE AUTHOR

Jason English lives in Boone, NC with his wife, Kimberly, and their two daughters, Grey and Violet.
He is the teaching pastor of a church family called theHeart.
He is also an Adjunct Professor of Public Speaking at Appalachian State University and a Visiting Professor of Biblical Studies at Charlotte Christian College and Theological Seminary.

This is his first book.

Go to **thingsaboutthings.com** for more things.

CPSIA information can be obtained
at www.ICGtesting.com
Printed in the USA
BVHW041740220719
554056BV00017B/783/P